WHISTLING DOWN THE WIRE

CLAUDE PELIEU-WASHBURN

translated
by
MARY BEACH

CHERRY VALLEY EDITIONS

Library of Congress Cataloging in Publication Data:

Pelieu, Claude.
Whistling down the wire.

Poems.
Translated from the author's unpublished ms.
I. Title.
PQ2676.E38A23   1977   843'.9'14   77-373
ISBN 0-916156-21-4

Typeset by Ed Hogan/Aspect Composition,
66 Rogers Ave., Somerville, Mass. 02144

Printed in the United States of America

*EVERYBODY AND
HIS UNCLE LOVES
SNOW'S CHOWDER*

WITH GOD
All things are possible!

*If you go to the States young
they become part of your culture*

*LOOK OUT MARS
HERE COMES MAN!*
The Old Farmer's Almanack

*Neige sur le désert. Cristallerie des fontaines.
Sur l'infini, jusque sur le ciel,
des chevaux et des Ford en liberté.*
Paul Morand

*Et sur la hanche
La signature du poète*
Blaise Cendrars

Outside. Forever outside.
Henry Miller

There's your money. Now get your ass out.
John H. Dillinger

I feel this is the comment
Andy Warhol

EASTBOURNE THE CITY OF TREES

to Mary

Clouds scud in an ocean-sky,
the moon barks in mauve mists,
and the sky all silver-proud suffused with orange & red,
long October shadows, rebel seaweed——
    Holywell, tamarisks, grassy knolls.
        lawns shining in the humid air——
    gaudy delicate flowers——Devonshire Park,
golf links & tennis courts, riders & cricketers,
    and in the distance majestic Beachy Head.

Hills encrusted with quick-silver enamel,
    rumbling thunder storms.
        huge eternal waves,
    and the sad song of the wind——firm even sands,
black pebbles & fine gravel——shipwrecked chalk
    orates in the floodlights.

Slopes planted with trees and wild flowers
    flower beds as blue
        as St. Sauveur's angels' baby teeth,
    the bright flower beds of the Grand Parade
            town houses, chalets, beach houses,
        bungalows & luxurious homes——Western Parade,
The Wish Tower, bandstands, esplanades carved right
    in the cliff, terraces and promontories,
        winding secret paths——healthy breezes
    stirring the golden broom & the spray
charming the multitude of birds hidden in the crags
    with floating stars, or in the bushes
        & in the grass.

Duke's Drive, Birling Gap, The Seven Sisters,
    green white & black,
        pressing hard on the landscape
Arcs of shadow & light cut in the cliff-face,
    and in the distance Cuckmere River all silvery
        stretching languidly in blue flashes——

4

West End, Paradise Drive——pier-promenade, tea-rooms,
    ball-rooms, bars & penny-arcades——
improvised windows of the past stirring the pre-war
    charms of by-gone days, flush with the windows
the City of Trees, vast stretches of velvet green,
    highrise buildings, shady terraces, illuminations,
        many-colored fairy-lights
            myriads of stars and regattas,
                slow hallucinations,
            shipwrecked photos & postcards.
And reality pressing down with all its weight,
    greasy papers, old rags, empty cans of Coke
        & comic books
    remind us that the 'holidaymakers' & their foul baggage
        have come & gone——In the bronze sky
the scintillating cascade of shooting stars crashes down
    ignoring the carnivals, the 'car-parks',
        ugly storefronts & the hordes of tourists,
            cartilage & displays of ugly fat——
Seaside Road, Zero Street, vestiges of the past when
        the bad taste of chips sets in,
        beckoning to the bronze statue
of the Seventh Duke of Devonshire.

Lonely early morning walks or late in the evening,
    Saffrons Road, Town Hall, Manor Park, The Meads,
        Marina Parade, horse racing, fox hunting, cocktail parties
    phantoms of smugglers & buccaneers——
St. Mary's Church still dominates Old Town,
    Hampden Park, Gildredge Park, South Fields, Temple Grove.
        South Downs——the half-erased history
            of the City of Trees where no one ever died
        for the pleasure of the blond mists.
Overlooking the sea & the landscape Anderida the Roman
    colony rising like a daguerreotype
        from Doomsday Book's red transistor.
Bourne in the widow of History's eye——Comte de Moreton,
    William the Conqueror, Edward the Confessor——
        blue sings under water & developed lyrical photos,
            the shadow's floating foam retains obscure complaints
        of sailors lost at sea, and the shipwrecked wind
            swallows great chunks of forest.

ROUND ABOUT MIDNIGHT

round about midnight
in the latrines of time
silence & death
sound the retreat

Round about midnight
flowers break
their solitude.

Under the great skies
where the half-dead
swarm, the wind weeps
& chrome bleeds.

Round about midnight
the vault of odors
erodes a flood of tears
boiling in a naked eye
denerved with dead skins.

Ultraviolet's electric
striped blondness lights up
the strange terror woven
by the wailings of the wind.
And syrupy sperm floods
night's great untidy gestures.

Round about midnight
if no one has seen
the wind, no one has lived
thru the fall of leaves.

A giant sore strips
the forest, & night
licks the saliva that
shines on a fingernail moon.

Round about midnight
colors tear at bibbed neon
with their teeth, scalping
the clouds & their cold songs.

Round about midnight
I couldn't care less.
My heart is gently
sloping, I was born
in frost, and I had
to forget something,
or someone. I had
to curl up.

Round about midnight
we furnished
the vacant lots
of the New World.
We searched & drifted
in present time &
we found nothing.

The shadow-mouth
sinks into the Milky
Way. The language G-string
sings like saw-teeth.
Snow ingots & empty
guts copulate in space
with photographic cells,
in a shower of sparkling comets.

Round about midnight
between heaven & earth
at 13,000 feet,
once more the sun rises
in the blackness of the blue.

Jacksonville-New York
Cherry Valley-London
Eastbourne-Paradise Alley

MURDER BY REMOTE CONTROL

To have seen a specter isn't everything...
              —Neal Cassady

Kiss the day goodbye, pal,
the crimson flowers
gargle behind
the white sky.

Used-Brain Dealer, just
follow your nose, shadows
impale empty
cemeteries. Shots, autopsies,
cremations, lips sponged off
with flames in Echo Park.
The Big Fix? Sex in
strange places. Shadow
Alphabet, Piss Factory.

Dawn, drawing of lots,
stopover sounds puked
out by darkness, exile
spray crushed by nerves,
Bingo Death. The blind
taste of flames on
the railroad tracks.
(Our working conditions
have turned dangerous),
the history of fire is
written in black letters
on San Miguel's white brow.
TO HAVE SEEN A SPECTER
ISN'T EVERYTHING,
masturbating the Death Machine
I say: Is America ready for
a good-time Fascism?
Hope so, it's a sort
of hobby. Dark reality
speeding on the Expressway.

Kiss the day goodbye, pal,
it's snowing, cold flows
without making a sound.
Captain Nark & the IRS
goons are waiting.
MASTURBATING THE DEATH MACHINE,
a good source of income.

Kiss the day goodbye, pal,
business as unusual, Old
Devil Moon says: 'I've a
King Kong size monkey
on my back'. On the dead
screen of summer nights
the sea ebbs, 'junkies are
safe in jail or in a
pine box' says the White
Death Horse.

*

Miracle rain falls in front
of the painted lips of dead
stars, Jayne Mansfield & Marilyn,
Buddy Holly & James Dean
appear between two clouds.
They used to shoot a lot
of B-Westerns out here.
Budding madness, salami-libido
in the trashcans of the wind,
fag-bodies preserved forever
frozen in cryogenized
nitrogen-ketchup filled
capsule at 80 below with
other human hamburgers.
Breaks & reefs, a sand storm
tramples on my reveries.

Our cat jumps into
a well of light,

I fall asleep after having
watched the late LATE Show,
spittle is nice & warm
in the Pony Express's
mail trunk/

Kiss the day goodbye, pal,
everything's burning
behind the horizon. Cold
weaves the wind's claws,
everything's burning
across the sky,
snowdrops turn blue
in the garden, the invisible
sleeps in the orifice
of darkness.

Kiss the day goodbye, pal,
chance-blades hear
everything, everyone
should understand this
in the ruins of the rain.
Mist trembles when
flowers fade, and numbers
are always right, it's
a healthy exchange.

Dead lesbians are at
the center of the debate.
Snow jumps over
every obstacle,
the colors of
the Indian Summer
are dying in
the sewers of secret
diplomacy.

A CIA guy put asbestos
threads in Manson's
wrinkled ass, Manson

the hostage of oblivion,
a pain-freak wandering
in the frozen area
of Death Row. Meanwhile
leftovers are recreated
and a smile floats
in the mud. Blood-music
(in the space-suit of
eternal light) is
preparing to ban eternity.

Gong-clots, acid-rock,
intrepid travelers,
ruin-seasons, vertigo-tufts
in the Milk Bar on
Patchwork Boulevard, kiss
the day goodbye, pal, dead
leaves yield to orange
neon, Autumn winds recruit
speechless voices.

*Friday afternoon,
all shared the same risk.*

THIS IS FOR ALL TIME REAL

WHISTLING DOWN THE WIRE, Calm Patchwork, Giant Nights,
the City's lights stir our slumber—night falls—seaweed green is
all golden. Mirror-masks flee time. Last night a strange silence
filled the bar. The image passed—huge wounds in the afternoon
—we're in the bed of sadness—bad news carved in the sky.
"We're alive! We're alive! I'll write it!" shouted the castaway
wandering in a skyless landless universe. Whether the world perish
or be saved shoulderless men no longer have the right to accuse—
Calm Patchwork, Giant Nights, elm & beech trees struck by light-
ning. Mirror-masks accomplices of a wordless death live, and the
great body of oblivion sinks in a blue lagoon—Fixed stars hang
from the odors of tamarisks, honeysuckle and winter jasmine—
blue green lawns, dazzling dew, fugitive echoes—Night falls.
Spray is placed on the horizon. The speed of damp mists, refugee-
sparks, emeralds, sapphires and colored stones like flowers dying
in clusters. Night falls. A bee dies in a bed of leaves.

WHISTLING DOWN THE WIRE, farewell to the Giants and wel-
come to the Standard Nightmare. Someone says: "We live in a
world of rapid change, and if we are to survive in such a world we
must be prepared to adapt." —NEWS FLASH: Banana Nose and
the Pope were caught with CBS crewmen jacking off on the roof
on a Brownie picture of Pat Nixon. . .Chairman Muff is dead,
'Death Row' Jeff is caught with Ernice Pressburger spitting in the
Big Boss's shit hole—after the police storm Attica, lawman 'Punk'
Jones says: "Hey! You whore! you've killed the Son of God in
your womb, you black bitch!"—It's during the worst moments
of war that cold is silhouetted behind you like the befuddled
laughter of a nigger. Images are filmed over a vacant lot on Riv-
erside Drive, a vacant lot wooded with hearts and—images buried
today under cigarette ashes. Popcorn and Sci-Fi, Angel Pussy and
fruit salad, grey cole slaw and hot chestnuts, films left in the flea-
bag rooms of the South Bronx—a last look at the ruins of the
Reality Studio and the skin of night murmurs: *We're like dead.*

Sparkling with dew wild flowers forget the danger, but the cold
waters of Death painted with light need the darkness—happy rac-

es are at the mercy of black crocodiles, viruses, noises and the Meat
Machine—Dazed zombies film the flight of time, everything crum-
bles, blood blurs the images, old claim-checks nibble at empty fac-
es and the City sleeps in a swarm of neon—the wind vomits fea-
thers and saliva. Dead gods sneeze. Farewell to the Giants, you
have to believe in Santa Claus cos' we're gonna rock rock ROCK
till the broad daylight—well, the old style 3-D is still faking the
fuck, so folks welcome to the standard nightmare.

WHISTLING DOWN THE WIRE, a blueish mica-anxiety on the
edge of the eye. The man in the street, the dregs-man sniffing at
keyholes and all the hateful mob, grotesque and mindless that al-
ways looks sideways to see in which direction the wind is blowing.
That hideous white voice devouring slogans that reap the farts of
the man-of-all-work who cools his heels in front of the Bureau of
Ideas and talks like a dead man—trashcans turn pale, the *rue
Sans Joie* pukes the garbage of the Oblivion Publishing Houses—
the wind frees red waves breaking over the forest. Goons separat-
ed from each other investigating the divided universe of perverts
are dying on the Jewish screen, and from time to time blood is
shed—Words are lost in the dark streets. Door-to-door word
salesmen come and go. Bloody shadows devour their hockers.
Dust in drag ends up by being dissolved in that neutral illegible
Western shattered in the glazed eyes of howling mobs—those who
never change color inject themselves with soot and shit—comets
murmur for the jukeboxes and vampires embrace keeping the Zero
Mental copyright that created these images and sounds. *Rue du
Point du Jour.* Liquid cash has the beautiful face of a night watch-
man.

Rue du Point du Jour
Oct 15, Poetry Day

TOWARDS A SKY DEVOURED BY MEAT

the dawn of a tattooed throat
        —Michel Bulteau

An avalanche of blue flames
on top of the hill, TEARS OF
SPACE ANGELS, cold bubbles
dying in Wog-bush with the lies
of Jerusalem and Commie/Papist
demons—broken films creaking
in the shadows—taxis meeting
in the violet twilight, and the silk
of the October sky lacerated
by pylons. The sexual parts of
Academic 'Critique' are crushed
on the Highway of Night.
A halo of skin unbuttons
the infinite. The dead are
evacuated by the mob.
The carrion-populace has voted.
And now what?—I'm talking
with scar-shadows & tattooed
stars—nature grazes
the eye-breaks of White
Technology—the sea pukes up
losers, bums, derelicts & the weak,
and those fools think things
have changed, sky-furnace
says: NO!!!

*

POETRY A LA CARTE
(IT SEEMS HISTORY IS TO BLAME)

to the Old Space Ranger

And already the last
of the Whites don't dare
open their mouths, I say:
Well, apartheid or not,
as long as we have
our health. . .Sicky sweet
vomit on the screen,
technicians vanish near
the lake of broken
razor blades, a star lashes
out at the ether-fringes
around the airport.
Silence is golden and it
will be the word of
my end——snow licks
railroad tracks, daybreak,
a storm marks time
in a swift erasure, veins
explore jungles torn
from North/South images.
Lotus leaves & poppies,
Krishna's fingernails,
Kali Yug's old panties,
and neon swallowing
germ-imprints. Silence!
Next page.

*

A STEP AWAY FROM THEM   (Frank O'Hara)

Who knows the secret of life & death?
Ain't nothin' stoppin' us now?
Bum rap, a long weekend as black as oblivion,
old faded spooks watching the stars fall,
old/young people frozen in despair, dreaming
of getting out of here. What's goin' on?
I dunno, a bum rap, that's all.
Riot police in Cities, civil and race wars,
legions of hookers, pushers, muggers, weirdos,
pimps, bionic assholes, punks, midgets, fags,
geeks, Spic-pricks, skunk-pussy eaters, businessmen,
working class scum, you name it! Power, Politics,
Crime, Money, Welfare, TimESPace, Showbiz, Art,
Talent, ping-pong, Poetry, cocksucking summers,
just guess Who's the Greatest?
A long weekend fucked up by Autumn's fire,
as black as oblivion and the slowness torn up
by neon. Ain't nothin' stoppin' us now?

*

MESSAGE

to David Bowie

The sky's speechless traps
envelop silence

Snow & gong-bones, soul-lines
like a wave shattering
& undertow-fever, & now
to set this filthy world
on fire David Bowie
tears up a white rose.

A cabin in a milky sky,
where the electronic
cathouse shines with
a thousand lights.
Explosions of tenderness.

We will travel in space
in shirt sleeves. Look!
the screen is a life-line,
a cathodic tidal wave
on a prank that went wrong.
NIGHT HAS THE MANNERS
OF BAD DREAMS, says the poet
in a tension-overflight,
I add: LISTEN PUNKS! AIN'T
THIS THE WAY ROCK 'N' ROLL
IS SUPPOSED TO SOUND? BOZOS!

*

FROM DARE DEVIL CREEK TO BEACHY HEAD

to Mary

if you want to know where God is, ask a drunk.
                    —Charles Bukowski

'I BECAME A MEMBER OF A SATANIC CULT AND
WITNESSED HUMAN SACRIFICES BY DEVIL WORSHIPPERS
WHO HOLD RITUALS ACROSS AMERICA'

                              True Detective

*

Nothing matters anymore.
Nothing. . .that day the wild iris wept, Autumn's round shapes
needed a vacation, God wept on the open piano with Sam Spade
. . .dead leaves embarked upon your shadow-drowned eyes. . .Old
Angel Midnight is writing again with broad mouth-strokes on the
moon-skiffs of El Camino Highway.
The stars come from far away in a budding sky.
Blood flashes in jukeboxes, eyes swimming in tears, silent images
on the ocean's skin, shadow-sounds die in the heart of New York,
the planet's asshole.
"But poetry is dull, very dull, so dull that the dullness is taken for
hidden meaning—the meaning is hidden all right, so well hidden
that there isn't any meaning", says Buk—well, I've never seen Sir-
ens on the banks of the Thames, I've only seen Turner's bloody
mouth and the steely eyes of a swordfish with the shriek of a sea-
gull. . .in the meantime I threw a lot of bull around.

*

The mystical brute reads the Baghavad-Gita in Yiddish, the mater-
ialistic derelict drifts around in the tense realm of supply and de-
mand.
Art? Well, it ain't for tha poor! Art is power money and talent.
That day Sheriff 'Punk' Jones was emptying the trashcans of his-
tory and I thought of the slaps that would be lost on future gen-
erations; foetuses tossed in the 'bidet' of History, enough to make
the stars cry.
That morning near the brimming garbage pails of broken bones and

masses of Western Union telegrams rotting on the river bed. Neon
shards took off and on the pier a sailor wept, a drop of blood dried
on the window-pane, blue grass had grown over the bridle path and
many-colored death with its satin claws trembled with fear.

*

Night swallowed a bouquet of white roses.

*

Dogs barked and wild cats snarled on the side of the road.
Pheasants, grouse and quail flew across a red copper sky.

*

Hollyhocks, sunflowers, wild iris, blueberries, primroses, corn-
flowers and forget-me-nots as far as the eye can see.
Shadows swollen with caresses.
Black butterflies watch over the archipelagoes of flesh.
Exile-souls sit on the edge of the lake.
Wind and dust. Pearly horizons. Great tides of blood.

*

Fear-flakes drift in the sky.
Disjointed skull-photos.
Pictures of civil war.
Niggers grimacing on walls of flesh. . .huge flowers in the tobacco
fields suffused with blond mists.
Festooned suns.
Distant stars twinkle and flash.
Balls of fire crash into the windshield.
And there's a boiling mass of sex behind the 'American Dream'.

*

DEATH ON ALL FRONTS—it all resembles a German silent film
of the 30s and innocence lost in electric blue groaning under the
whip lashes of desire. . .*the dream?*—in September 1620 one hun-
dred and four Pilgrims embarked on the 'Mayflower', one hundred
days later in December 1620 one hundred four men women and
children landed at Plymouth Rock, and they were to found the
future U.S of A. The sky puked fateful dates, and in the softness
of the evening they sang in light years.

(The French, who, long before had roamed over the future states
were decimated when Montcalm and Champlain died. And *that*
was *that* for 'La Nouvelle France'.)
A sad song and a flash of gong-antenna scent.
Now, the Deep South——a black moonless night——it was hot and
the crickets sang merrily.
Flickering images hanging onto what is left of life, photos in the
rearview mirror.

*

And that peach-colored sky over the St. John's River, Jax, Fla. A
twinge in my heart threw me back into the present.
Pink clouds still dance in the eyes of a chick killed on the highway.
Debris of flesh-filled light in the rearview mirror.
We're in an interval world.

*

Sitting in the garden in the shade of the palm trees I glance over
the newspaper headlines.
'A BOMB IN BUTTERMILK ROAD'...Screw the Irish. Screw
Ireland!...Something is happening...she is singing and holding a
bunch of wild iris in one hand, she has red hair and an electric flag
floats behind her lips...she is not twenty...the weather is fine...
An explosion erases it all.
Armed men advance hugging the walls and the crustaceans are yak-
king about *revolution*...
You have the right to weep under the weight of absence when a
wordless death flickers under the phosphorescent wheels of the
Snow Subway.

*

That day a sprig of wild mint masked the back country...and I
walked in the darkness in ruined streets.
Metallic sounds under a blue shower. Dead echoes on walls
bleached by the Florida sun.
It is hot, very hot. The golf course is all white and it's snowing in
a young girl's eyes.
A scarlet trolley rumbles across Silver City.

*

Lasso-mists groan in blood's imagined mud.
The moon rises like an anchor.
A tube of neon explodes, a murder and the shriek of a seagull with
broken wings.
A police chopper whirrs over the garden.
The sidereal immensity suffused the unkempt mosaic of the sky.

*

Comets imprisoned in a bone sky——famine-holes in the grey dawn
——flowers swollen to bursting point in the Florida sun, hicks go
off to the fields and a nog jacks off in the stables.

*

Electronic architecture, neon scaffolding, studded stars and the
ocean's skin sizzles...insects buzz...gusts of wind carry away the
leftovers of time.
Hard and soft sounds come to die on the beach, on the sunny side
of the street.
A cardboard Western, fragile shadows are ambushed in time's sil-
very capsules.

*

Street punks, bums, Kommies, jerks, turd-twisters, cocksuckers
and the Teenage Asshole of the Year——a buncha losers!——what's
left for them? Nothing except maybe speech, and all they do is
stutter, the mindless fools!...Wild mint drips on the black stones
at Dare Devil Creek...a Romeo and Juliet silence over a field of
photos.

*

Holograms near the gas-station at Paradox Lake——odors of gun-
powder and blood in the crappers at the UN——and over there, in
a vacant lot, the negative of the 60s and 70s, a Soap Opera of Sil-
ence and Death.

*

America is submerged in filth!
Lord! At last we're an ethnic minority!...Thus spake Bwana-
Thustra!

*

Very early on Monday in Cherry Valley, the sheriff picks up the
garbage on Fagola Street. Chas thinks it's a gas!
Honey Boy Bongo says: "LET'S FACE IT, MAN, DEATH
SELLS!"

*

Shadows of Cherry Valley enshrined in the snow.
Man-eating machines.
And further on the city and all its aggressions, a source of life and
passion. . .violence and aggression, every living being's a constructt-
tion game. . .Can you assholes deny it without denying life itself?
Just look at the waste they've made of their lives. . .

*

I was born in the region where white wheat grows under a vague
moon bathed in laughter and agony——here, words puked out by
hate need no translator——famine-holes, the birth of the Universe
. . .to make those fools laugh you have to put yourself in degrad-
ing and humiliating situations.

*

"Chas, if you had a balcony you could throw money to the poor",
I told him, and went on: "But what's the use, they're the only
ones who can afford to buy goods cheap."

*

Someone murmured: WHERE ARE THE NIGGERS OF YESTER-
YEAR?——a poppy-sun as red as the solitude of Mississippi, as
white as Beachy Head's profile, as the traces of lightning.

*

Shit! Winter is here!
Soul-flesh crushed by a thousand sufferings.
Word-batteries. Cassettes of laughter and images. Cartridges of
emotion. Colorless and timeless loud voices.

*

Winter is here as round as an anvil.

*

The soul is X-rayed by the weight of words against the sky.
Nerves and blood are on the summit.
And now the cocksucking snow...

*

I remember that one evening when the light was slowly fading an
electric knife cut thru the sun and it died in the ferns at Anderson
Creek. Then came a side-swipe from the rain like a red spot in the
white grass—and I saw the tourists and the Medicare people, tech-
nocrats, baboons, robots and proles scale pyramids of dirty linen—
the Maestro of Mediocrity is in seventh heaven, in a trance speak-
ing about events that could change the course of history.

The fucker was a born loser like a French Leftist wading hap-
pily in ideological excrement and the lousy crowd made every con-
cession of left-wing shortsightedness and violence imitating reality.

*

In New York we bumped into a few old friends.
Nerves in their orlon prisons no longer believe in miracles.

*

Raising his glass Dr. Goodwin Batterson Beach murmured: "One
cloud doesn't necessarily make it rain", then he told us some jokes.
Bonamicus Actensis was preparing to die, serenely and with a lot
of humor. He had lived a century and had lived well. He had seen
everything. He was a 'Son of the Mayflower'. He was as white as
the giant birch tree in his garden, as red as the maple, and he calm-
ly contemplated the mess in which *his* America seemed destined
to expire.
The yellowed pages of his books were turning blue in a Zane Grey
Dawn.
Ave atque vale!
Night flowers caress the jagged rocks of New England—visions of
centuries, of milleniums—bones burned on light's skin. Black
cold strikes down image-bodies.
No one knows how to read seaweed anymore and he deplored it.
On a backdrop of night death's game punctuated life's script. One
evening in West Hartford he read seaweed among the trees, an H
bomb plowed thru his gaze and emotion lost its rain check.

*

Lunch with Bill Burroughs on Canal Street at 'Luigi's' the Wop's
joint. Bill wore green sneakers like my special agent Joe Vermi-
nex.
Impossible to get Carl Solomon on the phone. So I sent him a
starched Jewish fish.

*

Ben Gay, the fish-queen and editor of the magazine *'Modes & Tra-
velos'* who won the prize 'Teenage Asshole of the Year' was out-
raged when I told him that every time shit becomes important, the
poor are born without assholes.

*

I hope that one day poetic art will become useless because I still
ignore the meaning of words. For example: *Politics, détente*—
inert details, democratic grimaces—the UN has turned into the
Theater of the Absurd.
Thank God words don't have the power to recreate the world.

*

A democratic gesture that pleases me: *WORKERS ORDERED TO
DISPERSE!*

*

The wind of the night wrings heart and soul and defoliates the
mind with the blow of an axe.

*

I had reserved a room at the 'Royal Armpit Hotel'. Mary had left
her suitcase in her room, and an hour later a Puerto Rican prick
had ripped her off of some worthless possessions.

*

New York Poetry 'Caf'Conce' cheek to cheek—Fagola Street—
God! People do have problems!....well, man, the asshole the
prick and the cunt coexist taking root in the biological event. ...
Hedonists and Eugenicists need to beat their meat in the morning
before starting the day, like the Nazis and the Bolsheviks they
want to destroy the nuclear and biological family.
Guts full of come hoisted on top of the Empire State building

creak explode and puke their shit into the ocean.

Soul-thieves and inspired archivists, regular customers of the *'pis-soir'*—lots of jacking off in the massage parlors of the Oriental Bazaar and they meditate staring at a sky studded with dirty enema bulbs—sexual anti-liberty invades bodies and minds, hits the Creed of the Circumsized, the Swan Song of the pudless pecker, the Hula of the Half-Witted Half-Breed.

It's not the time for miracles in the great jungle that is our lives. The poet is not always absent from life, he uses it, observes it and tames it and the words topple into Dr. Reich's orgone box.

*

Lifetime?

Huge blocks of spontaneous prose, autobiographical or not—the writer barely lives, he observes—and it all hangs out as soon as the Choirs of the Subconscious remember and the sexual vendetta continues in the streets.

*

Silence vibrates in the darkness of space.

You can *see* it.

Life's record is scratched and the poet uses a ladle to smear his ass with ketchup.

*

Silhouetted against the sky the future is daubed with blood mud and shit. People talk. They seem to be created for the sole purpose of talking on and on to the end of time.

*

Cold blurred photos—James Dean 1931-1955—Porsche petals in the dew, he left everything to follow a spark. A finger waggles in sea-writing. Bodies and souls are no longer featured in the sunset credits.

*

Cherry Valley-Montreal—we arrived at Kulturburger City (Mary, Pam, Elizabeth and Chas)—the Yogi and the Commissioner heard that Manson's 'Family' intended to kidnap (among others) Frank Sinatra and to skin him alive. So, it seems that those charming

young people, the vanguard of the 'counter-culture' would sell
Frank's skin to the 'head shops' and 'psychedelicatessens', so
everyone could have a little piece of Frank.
Now, since we've seen the greasy bum Arafat at the UN with his
pistol in his belt nothing astounds us anymore.

*

The President of the Sperm Bank and the Zionist Asshole vanished
in the Egyptian mist somewhere around Longueil.
Suziki, the Fag and a Khmer Rouge patted the pig the Montreal
hicks had given them, the derelicts of the 'counter-culture' camped
in the Oval Office at the White House waiting for the arrival of an
interpreter. Isabelle Ladouceur and Gaetan Vadeboncoeur delous-
ed each other under a portrait of Lincoln, assisted by a dazed
pimply IRA hood who stood to one side sweating Guinness.
'Stinking Cloud' and 'Fuck Buffalo' the token Indians read Brecht
together. A poet sputtered into the mike: "The Khmers Rouges
have done a great job". A puny Chilean started to tweek his gui-
tar. A purple flash erased them giving them all their proper politi-
cal dimension.

*

I was very upset. I had already seen the same filth ten years be-
fore in New York and Frisco.
Did I say upset? Actually I regretted Florida and New England...
the golf courses, swimming pools, motels and colonial mansions
—America was submerged in filth and stupidity—THE SECOND
COMING OF THE DIRTY HAIRY WHITE JERK.
And I remembered our escape to New York in a powerful Buick
with Mary and Bull D. Brau.
We drove for eight hours without going flabby and when we ar-
rived in Gotham City the filthy old fil was still unwinding over the
sad ghetto.
Sky-rinds, grease spots, dog shit, Puerto Rican snots, sexual rumors
in the nigger streets.
"Honor & Prairie! Better Tex than Mex!" cried the Texas Ace
while he assfucked Speedy Gonzales.

*

Well, ten years later they had 'discovered' grass, acid, rock 'n' roll,

this, that, the 'class struggle', the Third World, mindless ventrilo-
quists and lice-ridden mystics, the saddleless bike, Women's Lib,
ecology, etc...Bravo!...they deserve a nice hand...politics and
promiscuity—Bourgeois terrorists have never had a sense of hum-
or, neither have the Communists, but that day in Saigon men pre-
ferred fire to Socialism. It was sad. Catatonic hippies spat in my
fruit salad so I said: "Speak you white motherfuckers! And give
my regards to Maria Chapdelaine!"

*

Papi Tomato talked to the angels about God always praising Him
to the skies. Adam Street and Johnny Saint smiled as they sat
contemplating the scene from their adjustable seafoam armchairs.
Some wall-eyed stinker had the gall to say I was a CIA agent, a
redneck, a crypto-Nazi!—maybe, and why not?—so what?

*

The *rue Saint Denis,* a totalitarian 'hip' ghetto. Groupies, char-
women and anemic would-be bombers. And all the French gunk
stuck to their straw-filled wooden shoes—a kibbutz for Christ-
ians—the Swami's dirty briefs were marinating in 'Mouton Roths-
child' and the crappers weren't even segregated!

*

The Dream-Police is molded in turds and blood. We were at the
'Thinking Shit-Hole', the bastion for left-wing French-speaking in-
tellectuals the 'Craspect Crispés' or 'Squalid Squatters'—neon
studs in the sky carried away by the April mist—American melod-
ies, crates of freckles and beauty spots—words fell from my lips,
yes, they were jacking off on the carcass of the 'revolution', speak-
ing of 'independence' of the *French* Kerouac who hailed from
Quebec. Playing with themselves in front of Mme. Binh's portrait,
the fools chanted Uncle Ho's *poems* (sic)—The niggers of space
had invaded the washeterias.

*

Overheated sex-images riddled the Montreal skies and the vibrato
of desperate situations.
Suck! Squeeze! Blow!

*

Drag queens as ugly as pigs' asses caught in the family album.
Memories of Vancouver and Toronto.
Now, I'm dreaming under the mangroves in front of Ma Barker's
blue and white house.
The stars pale over Atlanta.
We're smoking on the veranda watching the tropical rain storm.
Images jostle each other. We drink ice cold vodka and smoke
Tampa cigars.

*

American images crash into the sky's windshield. The Black gard-
ener scratches his head a minute, retraces his steps and mutters to
himself that it's wiser to leave everything *blank.*

*

A wild wind chases the clouds over an archipelago of nerves.

*

A dream torn from God's fly is recorded by the poet's camera, but
nothing matters anymore—the St. Banana flying the Greek flag is
anchored in port—I watch the longshoremen and take photos.
Well, all I can say is that they're not the only ones who work like
Nee-groes.

*

The men lower the cargo in nets, hoist crates and bales onto wait-
ing flatcars and pickup trucks—cranes, trucks, monstrous vehic-
les, riot-sounds—Mr. and Mrs. Centaur leave the 'Wet Dream'
Club, the centauress is seen giving the rabbi head.
Messages jammed into rotting sleeping-bags.

*

We drink Bourbon with James, Paul, Chas, Victor, Sister Vaseline
and Diarrhea Montez—we're in a cassette ghetto—queers and
poets, midgets and broads. Chas points out Charlie Chan's obsid-
ian fly sticky with 'Southern Comfort' and smoked barracuda.

*

Shitty ghosts get stoned in some greasy spoon or other. No details
are left out by the zombies.

*

It's raining on the city.
Rotten light.
The garbage hasn't been picked up.
We think of our impending end.

*

Sister Mucus Welby MD and the dream-sower drift on a wrinkleless
cloud.
We rope stars with our lassos.
An anemic sun rises in a dirty dawn.
Top-dog turd manages an 'in' nightclub called the *Vocal Infection*.

*

DEATH ON ALL FRONTS——a boiling mass of sex——filmed life
marches in time. Sexual vendetta in the empty streets. 1776-1976
a dawn-putsch. Happy Birthday America!

*

The Twilight World and the leftovers of a silvery Western, broken,
laid out by speed and framed by neon and vanishing in a pool of
light.

*

In a jumbo-jet an air-hostess spots a hi-Jacker.
Two shots——the Cuban vanishes in a cloud of dry ice and kerosene
——dangerous scales between life and death when subhumans chew
on their meanness——real events and fiction intertwined. Much ado
about nothing in the stables of Thought.
Distant cries.
It's the end of the biological film.
I aim straight at the faggots hustling in the cold darkness, I aim at
the red roses in their lipless mouths.
The monsters digest the dead roses.
Not so long ago I was flying over the Great Plains of the West——
huge flesh checkerboards and junkyards——a musical comedy, a tot-
al spectacle, cartoons and horror films.

*

The shriek of a seagull pierces the purple fog and over there I see the docks, warehouses, sailors' bars and real moving ships.

*

Back in Europe. . .the same creeps. . .Red bureaucrats grabbing
everything little by little.
Look over there, on the corner, childhood is swallowed by a bomb
by a grenade by a blast of machine-gun fire—the 'freedom fight-
ers' have done it again—and the words echo in the trashcans in
Chinatown full of dead cats and dogs.
A black tide threatens Beachy Head.
A silvery life-line over its green and white cliffs.
The meeting will come to order—*Bang! BANG! You're dead!*

Oct 3, 1656, Capt Miles Standish d.
USA-UK, 75/76

EXILE ON MAIN STREET
(A NEW DECLARATION OF INDEPENDENCE)

to Michel Bulteau

The sun is bleeding over the sky!
          —Philip Lamantia

LATE WEATHER FLASH:
hard rain, rolling thunder and idiot wind.

Gold trickles in cats' eyes.
The whiskey is good. The magic seeds are thirsty. Silence bleeds
a little. Losers are left stranded by the wayside, and some anemic
punks are still playing with Death in the halls of the Snow Subway.
Poets aren't social workers.

Death scores like Dope and Sex.

Swirls in the steel and cement jungles—young flesh that the no-
tion of sin floors when the blueness of childhood jumps feet first
in the mud—Kojaculation! Boozarama! R 'n' R crap! Burger
Time Machine! Instant Poetry!

Pregnancy is a Jewish plot.

How to get a foothold?
Bubbles, snowy tears, night falls on Gun and Thunder Hills.

There's something you can't imagine. I have proof—a phospho-
rescent tongue stirs the night—Proof, baby?—I don't argue about
things like that. Who gives a fuck? I strike out, I shoot, point
blank. Super redneck, that's me folks. That's me, no tolerating
the myopia of nerves.

Silver ashes in the pink window and the colorless veins of a gener-
ation weep in the darkness.

Exile on Main Street. The Planetary Zoo and its rabble haven't
much time left.
White sounds grafted on rumors of civil war electrified by Simian
imprints.

Strangled waves—poems and songs bubble with joy under the Buc-
caneer's lash—an eddy of blood covers the scenery masking an
ageless sky.

What do the waves say today?
They say: "Smoked meat and green thunderbolts."

Vague rumors from mouth to mouth. Shit kneels down, nerves
creak with madness-crystals under time's devouring caresses.

Tension-network.
The endless sound of worlds.
Flocks of tears.

*

Wasps Attack Fete

FLORENCE, Sept. 17 (UPI).—
Wasps stung about 100 spectators
at a Communist festival here last
night, police said.

___

INNER LIGHTS OVER BEACHY HEAD

Nirvana? Heaven?
X? Whatyoucallit?
—Jack Kerouac

Chablis, wild strawberries,
Devonshire cream, ginger bread
and nauseating French ballads,
dawn is full of black sighs.
Inner lights over Beachy Head,
the world is obliterated
by unfeeling dead metal.
Dead leaves avoid meat
hanging in the windows. Black
& Red Autumn gnaws at
the keys of memory. Great
starry shadows vanish
in the pastel blue of dawn,
a white dream stitched
with frost.

*

STATION TO STATION

Learning to see the aggressors
As huggable, kissable idealists.

And their eyes dim slowly,
like those intangible pages
in transit at the frontiers of space.
Space Opera, light years swallow
torrents of obscenities, the sun
still hot at this time sinks into
seaweed, every sorrow is curtailed,
the grass is greening on
the golf course, and the moon
bathes the blue grass screams.
Mr. Mandala lets out a tickled
broad's giggle; Sterling is falling,
the Simian Dildo-man devours shreds
of white skin, howling hot metal
neglects evolution, and attacks the
freckles of the survivors.
A storm causes floods downtown.
The flabby bellied unemployed
come out of fetid sewers,
their features express complacency
lost in the steppes of sex,
flying over radioactive crossbred
landscapes, their eyes dim
slowly. Life melts in the mouth
of those who spread lies and death.
Phosphorescent images float in the air.

*

to Mary

*'We're sure going to
have some wrecks now'*

I remember over Rainbow
Bridge we became holograms,
3-D of the future, all done
with lasers. I remember
thru those funny decades
refusing to become a suck-ass
I walk tonight
on an empty stage.
An oblique shadow erased
the TV Studio, Summer of '76,
Paris, howling metal-death
transforms the streets
spattered with blood.
I remember the Hungarians
next door shitting
on the stairs. Klieg lights
halo this unique tragedy,
& invading night tames
electric dust. The Blacks
are already at work,
silence moves, noise grabs
at cursed facts, & I play
with the sky's pebbles

*July 26, St. Anne
Dog Days, New Moon*

*

ROUND ABOUT MIDNIGHT FLICKERING FINGERS
DIE IN SAND CASTLES AND TAKE ON THE COLOR OF RUST

The echoes of these decades frozen in silo-archives of slag-
    anthologies couple with the grimaces of a generation that
    barks its age.
There is nothing left. Administrative prose, occasional verse,
    trivialities. There is nothing left except a few sex-flakes
    winking in the tangerine sky.
The cold holds me back. Night has nothing to declare. Neon is
    famished. It's all the same to me.

Round about midnight the dream-kayak is carried away by
    a morgue-echo into a bone-jungle,
and silence follows bite-sounds into eye-hallways.

Round about midnight I disembowel flowers, and the clear
    water of tresses embroiders with clenched fists.
    Winter scissors say that war is imminent, and the wind won't
stop it. Freckles are astounded by nothing.
    The language of flowers is opposed to us. A century of smoke
    carved in water, and a shadow as wide as a river.

*

FEELINGS

Yesterday a hurricane
bleached the red hot landscapes.
FROST BIT A TANGO-COLORED MOON.

Jolly nerves flood
the pinball machines
flickering with flesh & bones
in the shadows, uncoupled screams
race down the highway
veering with UNHINGED TINFOIL
IN INFERNAL PLAYTHINGS.

I will never be the bolt
of hostages says the poet
walking on the gold fish
sealed by McLuhan.
BLUE STARS DISINTEGRATE
IN THE SKY.

IT'S THE STAGE OF THINGS TO COME

to Chas Plymell
poet, stuntman, novelist,
starfucker, cowpoke
keep 'im flyin'

All is in order.
There are no regrets
to have, 'but being
a poet is an anomaly,
there is no justification',
take it and flow my tears,
drifting above the freeway
thinking about what
Bomkauf, the Abomunist
said dying on the road:
"Look at them, look
at them! They're full
of shit! Stay out there,
man, and out of it!"
Since then the planet's
time has been upset,
the dead astronauts
have been embalmed.
It's the stage
of things to come,
so, get lost phonies,
fucking poets, con-men,
lousy radicals,
bad-asses, street punks,
aging queens, creepy
crawly Kommies
& Red Dykes lost
in the tundras
of sex, go to hell!
What authentic thing
have they ever
demanded of life?

Eternal yahoos,
geeks sputtering
in electrified dust,
afraid of the blue
laughter of the
Morning Star.
All is in order.
I regret nothing,
because every mile
of the Highway
of Night is numbed
by Poetry, no regrets,
but my life is
from now on
so unimportant that
I don't want to die.
As Mary says: "A half
hour's cooking time
& boredom burns
your guts out."
The wind persists
in chewing up one town
after the other.

Oct 28, 1776
The Battle of White Plains, NY.

FROZEN DEATH

(poem from Journals & Stories)

*to Rusty Jack Greywood, Paul Grillo
& Howard Hughes*

"I may go down sometimes but
I always come back rocking"

The middle of nowhere
is a very private place.
Everything seems like
yesterday, and we are out
of control, the Mobfuck comes
out of the Time Tunnel.
What is left of the Videotheque
of the Universe? Nothing,
except for a cafeteria
The Nog Queen Kosher
Parlor, an electrified
sex-butcher shop.
The Time Guide crumples
between his phosphorescent
fingers a faded photo
of James Dean. Don't look back,
I may go down sometimes but
I always come back rocking.
light flakes in an iron
grey sky. Freckles drift
in the raw light. Blue flames
in the chimney, snowdrops,
crocuses, primroses,
and the green shoots
of daffodils; the thaw,
it's the end of winter.

Faded photos swirling
in the streets of the past,
kinky nignogs jacking off
in the orange neon,
the biological film

40

grimaces in the hollow
of a song, recoil
of Winchesters in the blond
streets of Silver City,
and on the beach a message
found in a bottle:
STILL ON DECK WITH A FEW
PEOPLE. ONE IS A CHILD.
THE LAST BOATS HAVE BEEN LOWERED.
WE ARE SINKING FAST.
THE ORCHESTRA IS STILL
PLAYING BRAVELY ON. SOME MEN
ARE PRAYING WITH A PRIEST.
THE WEATHER IS BEAUTIFUL.
THE SEA IS CALM.
THE END IS NEAR.
THE ANGELS ARE SINGING.
MAYBE—THIS—NOTE WILL
The satellite 'Sleeping
Blue Note' is lost
in a black velvet sky,
with hunks of stars
& sun shards, the Chasm
Gang produces the last
Space Opera: THE WRONG END
OF TIME. The past is more
and more like fiction
and lets grace burst forth.
Image-streets & tragedies
in a pool of sky hell is built.

*

YES, WE HAVE NO NIRVANAS

Broken moons.
Bone fogs.
Neon radar in
the American Dream.
The sirens of police
cars make dead dogs howl.
Walk tall *whoever*
you are, walk tall
& stop looking, yes,
we have no nirvanas.
We're like dead, you'd
better believe it.
It's a grand
circle-suck,
& everybody
needs a mouthful,
& then deep-throat
it in extremis,
& curtain!
Neon. Echo
of live flesh.
Images buried
in Nigger streets.
Rainbow-sounds
behind the budding
stars, the curtain
falls raising
a soul-fog.
Stop looking.
Image-fits rolling
from chasm to chasm.
Walk tall & groove
high, bananas aren't
created equal.

Oct 14, 1066
The Battle of Hastings

*

WHISTLING DOWN THE WIRE

to Bomkauf
a.k.a. Old Angel Midnight

Poetry News That Stays News

Whistling down the wire
with God on our side . . .
smoke-tatters
licking at space,
loud splinters erasing
earth-films shot by
angels of Paradise, howling
in the Apocalyptic din,
fleeing solitudes,
demon-ambulances. . .
mutilated tortured bodies,
bloody stumps, ruins
& garbage skyward. . .
the shadow grows dense,
becomes knife-like. . .
Whistling down the wire
in a free fall, with
no rhyme nor reason. . .
Did we intend to die
like this? . . .
Bare chrome hands
burned alive on a carpet
of kites, crumpled eyes,
forget-me-nots staring
at the Stars' Flour Mill. . .
with God on our side
sun spots still play
over Panorama City
in the shadows, a Ford
pickup truck crashes
into the plate glass window
of thought. . .smoke-tatters
scratch at the rearview
mirror neon sunflowers
& tufts of water.

ETERNITY IS A LONG WEEKEND, *NOW WHAT?*

Images & sounds
rush into the empty
cold dangerous streets,
folded streets,
dead streets, SICKNESS
AT THE RIVER OF THE SKULL,
and snow erodes
the bluelit night.

*

FLOWERS BURN *RUE DU POINT DU JOUR*

In two hours we'll be flying
from NY to London in the air
crowded with fear. Bouquets
of mist, stubs, rains, confetti,
rainbows, China Dogs perched
on distant waves, colored specters,
old objects rotting in grey
mildewed rooms of a country
that is no more than a tomb.
Flowers burn *rue du Point du Jour,*
black sand weeps at the bottom
of a lake of blood.

*

THERE IS NO MORE LAND!

223 West 55th Street,
blisters, Xmas carols,
xerox pranks, white turds,
Black pimps, creeps,
comatose halfbreeds
sniffing the yellow sky.
We were rich, of our
own accord, as white
as crystal, we came out
of music & dreams,
white civilized slaves
dancing in a blazing
street, and God was
scratching His ass,
sex took pot luck
under the sky's
indigo vault, with
fuzzy blue
nigs floating
in the pink sulphuric
twilight, hideous
metallic howling
tortured & a neutral
night closed over them.
A voice off stage
put out the lights
straddling the razor's
edge. A white sky with
acacia thorns smeared
with sweat: THERE IS
NO MORE LAND!

*

COLLAGE-POEM

to the Polaroid-Buddha,
the Code-Breaker
And for Carl Weissner

Wait a minute, pal. We're walking the wrong way.

Tense images, wounded words choking on Diesel fumes
    on the Locust-Planet.
The parking lot's yellow grass trembles in the blue light.

Jukeboxneons, rolls of plasticized flesh, phone booths
    papered with hockers, sick bodies spinning in the orange
    neon,
stamping on asphalt incrusted with dead eyes.

Cowpoke Blues, Rock Dreams, Honky Tonk Angels singing sad
    songs, choking on Diesel fumes on the Locust-Planet...
a rainbow of penny-arcades & jungle-gyms...twenty years
    drifting, for what? *Because...*
Shit! Enough of that!...we all need to love someone, especially
    when a blue sun digs up torn streets,
& motels & gas-stations explode on the language-road.

A voice off stage introduced us to a nowhere that laughs
    without a sound,
hologram-images sizzle forever in jelly capsules.

*

HOWARD R. HUGHES

to Mickey Spillane

The stars resembled blood stains,
spattered flesh-negatives burned
to ashes, fade-in chained to the voice
dust of Oak Street, Farewell Blues,
strangled acid sounds, distant voices
in the cold air so calm & blue.
We're not their judges
We're their judgment. I'm the hunter
& my price is death. My services
cost too much, always a good reason
for lettin' a man go, said
the Widow-Maker at Smackass Pass
overlooking Pee Dee River.
"Big Brother is small potatoes next
to Howard. He might be watching YOU,
but you can bet that Howard would
be watching HIM"—we don't have
the means to live without killing,
psalms & slaughter, anti-riot photos,
gigantic waves laughing quietly
soft sounds like the soughing of wind
in trees—a necessary end?
Back from Death Mike, sex-shards
planted in neon, Zipper Puke sold
sexy messages in the streets
of Silver City, images passed
& repassed in front of my eyes
with soul-wrinkles & cloudbursts
which fell from the sky in a dream.

Razor Burn Station, 4 p.m.

*

APRIL IN PARIS

Well, the reefer make you move too slow

I don't know why or because of whom, at the end of the after-
noon, I found myself in a small cemetery in Paris. It is true I had
had a lot to drink. And I was to be in Paris for such a short time,
I had so many things to do, so many assholes to see. Well, the
reefer make you move too slow. It was an unusual kind of drunk-
enness——I saw dead children flattened against a wall of broken
bones covered with ivy, Virginia creeper and honeysuckle——Lords
and new Creatures stirred in the single universe.

I felt like praying. My eyes were brimming with tears.
Filthy phantoms tore at the quicksilver screen.

Music of strange days attenuated by a wave of light whiskey.

Merry-go-rounds, bandstands, beggars, wild strawberries, vanilla
icecream and mint lollipops——fragile old ladies in black and mauve
placed charming bouquets of flowers on the graves covered with
red and gold moss——a purple fog enveloped the pale silhouettes,
the metallic creaking of the silence trampled those old fashioned
specters in the alleys.

Drunkenness, dreams, music, soul-dust. Dead dogs drifted in the
sky.

I had the feeling I was being absorbed by a wave of tequila-valium.

Death would descend from the sky to shed the blood of poets in
the heart of the April light itself, the clamors of death frightened
me. And yet I had seen quite a few people die——people I had
loved and people I hadn't even liked——I had killed for kicks——I
loosened my tie and took off my raincoat. Filthy squishy mouth-
sounds echoed in my ear. Paris looked like a fruit rotting in the
sun, an electrified 'Camembert'——I recalled the streets littered
with dog shit, wog snots and household trash, the repulsive crap-
pers in the bistros and in the private homes, the gaping hole that
replaced *'Les Halles'.*

That day I was in the *'Cimetière des Amants'* completely drunk, I
was in the cemetery where the *'Doux Guillaume'* was resting. The
Père Lachaise to be exact.

That day the silhouettes of death advanced with giant steps fol-
lowed by sparks.

For a long time poets had abandoned their sandbags and the Morn-
ing Star no longer slept in the grass.

Torrents of blood flooded the streets that smelled of civil war.

Distinctly I heard the screaming of mindless throngs spelling out
political slogans as if thru a wall of cotton wool.

+ + + + +

Thru a dense hot red mist as thick as blood, I saw the pioneers,
the colonists, the settlers, men of letters and musicians, the ships
and their cargoes of slaves, the visionaries, priests and soldiers,
buccaneers, lawmen, preachers, outlaws, boatmen, stuntmen and
buffoons; yes, I saw them all, men and women alike, take every
risk and create a new world——Time bled in its capsule——I saw the
hells and the paradises lost, I was revisiting a devastated universe.
I reorganized the silence and human sounds and then a spaceship
sank into the black snow and I was wafted up to the stars.

For a moment, getting my balance, I thought those outbursts of
feeling were risky and somehow out of place so I decided to cower
in the heart of a prayer.

For several months, stoned or not, I would read over a few verses
of the Bible and I would say grace.

Under the faded flowers there broke a tidal wave of alcohol blood
and sperm——mirages, ruins, tombs, Catholic wedding cakes, extra-
ordinary monuments, myriads of meteors and French noises——an
April oath on the clayey strip of land.

I thought that rats were never surprised at the rigidity of death.

Suddenly all the waters of the oceans closed over the planet erasing virgin soil forever.

I was drunk and I knew that I would be taking a plane with Mary later. It was then I saw on a wooden signpost: WHEN YOU'RE DEAD IT'S FOR LIFE——it was Jim Morrison's grave——full speed ahead on the American Route to Romantic Martyrdom——had Jim been smarter he wouldn't be dead.

Twelve hours later in L.A., I heard that a friend had died in a mot- el in Pacifica as well as 'The Queen of the Highway'.

Swing-spasms in the cat's golden eyes.

A star pushed out of the window by the rain crashed in the sun's chromed wounds.

BLUE THE COLOR OF SILENCE——possible names for Death: 'String Quartet' or *'Joyeuses Enigmes'?*——what's happening to the film? Nothing, I take your word for it and I wake in a cool wind.

Blue Wasteland, hungry improvisations, stone sparks on the wind- ow-panes. The wind at Land's End speaks to the end of the earth. The mob's iron wings abolish the eloquence of blood——a sad song comes to my eye——I'm always sitting on the fire-escape aiming at the leathery rough lips of policemen——angels' silver fingernails break the jaws of the sky.

Flowered ruins and *'Joyeuses Enigmes'*, the wind's mouth makes forget-me-nots blush, and a girl stabbed the transistor hidden be- tween her legs——roses forgotten in a letter box on Black Oak Street——fractured light flowed out to sea.

Silence is a floating knife. Blue, the color of silence, a velvet ham- burger, the Big Fix, God's Spectral Eye, wounds creaking in the uprooted dawn——voice-blasts on the freeway——a door slams and birds fly over the waves and survivors take shelter in street caverns.

THE INTUITION-REVOLVER BARKED IN THE SHADOW—
DAWN-SHARDS OVER TOPANGA CANYON—THE NEON
LIGHTS ARE GOING OUT—AN INVESTIGATION IS BEGUN,
MURDER, SUICIDE OR ACCIDENT? WE WILL NEVER KNOW.

The grass's razor slit thru the daylight.

Paris, New York,
L.A., Eastbourne

COFFEE planter, Alonso Benivolo was furious when he learned that his beautiful young wife, Maria, had a lover.

He searched his plantation for a swarm of hybrid bees which he knew attacked without cause — and had already stung several people to death.

After a week, 50-year-old Alonso found the deadly swarm in a tree and put them into a box.

Then he drove to his home near Puerto Ayacucha, Venezuela, where Maria, 27, was in bed with her lover behind drawn curtains.

Alonso released the angry bees into the bedroom and locked the door.

Ten minutes later he opened it, armed with an insecticide spray. The lovers were lying on the floor, screaming with pain.

"They had been stung in the most delicate places and were rushed to hospital," said police.

Alonso, who was arrested on a grievous assault charge, said: "I got the idea because I used to call my wife Honey."

SLOW-MOTION EARTHQUAKE OVER RAINBOW BRIDGE

in memory of William Wantling
murdered a few years ago
By the White Death Horse
52

Hi Bill, Pooh loves you. . .you're in Heaven now. . .it's a nice place
to live if you're a shmuck, but you ain't a shmuck. . .Here a long
weekend as black as oblivion sinking into the veins of time. . .
Can't find your poems. . .Hope you're living in a clear sky in frost
and light. . .From here nothing to report. . .bad scenes, terrible cha-
os, worldwide inflation, civil wars, etc. . .Dope and Death still score
. . .I've been thru all that, fell asleep on a mattress of mildewed
Bibles left there, never opened. . .I've flown over every landscape as
you know, and daily life becomes tougher, easier, stranger, softer
and half-erased. . .Now I'm a camera bouncing in empty space. . .
My heart and nerves have spoken, then my head is crushed by the
sound of an era. . .slow-motion earthquake, I film the death of
legends and myths. . .the colors have gone, Bill, pieces of the puz-
zle are missing. . .You can't read my new poems and wild stories. . .
How are you?. . .I'm sure the path to Heaven isn't Death, but
you're dead smartass, and I'm alive. . .Recently the Meat Machine
swallowed many people. . .Yeah I know what you think: a fucking
bum rap for sure. . .yeah, but you're dead, dead, DEAD. . .Did you
know that our moon rings like a bell?. . .Take it easy, pal, so long
. . .and stay away from the 'Big Yard'.

*

A NECESSARY END

A Barbecue View of Daily Hallucinations,
ageless film, flesh-negatives on a wall
of paper roses, the credits explode,
nog-images stretched out like gum
in a jungle of old photos. Day breaks
on Technopolis. HORROR ITSELF IS OUT OF DATE.

*

COLORS BURIED ALIVE

Poets lose their heads,
upside down I'm writing
this in the Castle of Sickness,
with Sister Palfium, a broken
leg leers at the camera,
the horizon's linings rise
in the twilight setting
Beachy Head ablaze.

*

PATCHWORK POEM (WASHBURN'S NOTES)

*in memory of General Henry Dana Washburn, 1832-1871,
and of Thomas Moran, English-born artist and William H. Jackson,
photographer, and of all the surveyors, explorers, settlers, gunsling-
ers and lawmakers who made nowhere somewhere*

Come! Rush! Hurry. Don't wait for anything!

God is good to all of you, but you'll be better off without me.
The Holy Road is ended. Tracks spell MEAT.

Early life thru the Civil War, the Indian Frontier, the Sioux War,
the Nez Percé War—Old Oxbow dead-run in the River—Patch-
work Poem following the coyote—Autumn's blond imprints are
erased by purple waters.

Mountains of shadow and light—Firehole River (Wyoming), tree-
less valley, silent landscape, Fort Ellis (Montana)—Indians and
soldiers killed—Bull-team wagon bosses, mud holes, washouts,
dust, Indians and road agents—Flat Mountain Arm of Yellowstone
Lake, Steamboat Point, US SIGNAL CORPS, CROW INDIAN
AGENCY.

When guns speak DEATH settles disputes—up where the big
winds blow—Bear River City, the Little Big Horn Disaster—
Custer and his men dozed in a slough of mud and disgust—Re-
member the merciless Montana sun, the sun-bleached bones.

Indian Scouts called 'White Swan', 'Big Nose', 'Three Jesus',
'Round Jean'—green gallows, gusts of wind, Black Glass Moun-
tains, Mammoth Hot Spring Terraces—presidios, Fort Custer and
Fort Keogh (Montana), Fort Bowie (Arizona), old maps, drawings,
watercolors, etchings, notes, diaries—Fort McPherson (Nebraska),
Jefferson Barracks (Missouri)—snow mountains, fossil forests, un-
ique landslides, eroded basaltic lava flows, spectacular deep valleys.
Gros Ventre River, Pacific Creek, Two Ocean Pass, Teton Pass,
Snake River, Yellowstone River—heavy June snows, cowskulls
and meadowlarks—Sulphur Mountain, Falls of Yellowstone, 'Old
Faithful', Elephant Black Mountain, Hot Spring Creek—clouds
of spray, tall rock spires, beautiful cascades hidden in the dim light

of over shadowing rocks and woods.

Yellowstone Canyon and Mount Washburn, Hot Pools—Turquoise, Jewel, Beryl, Opal—the deep valley of the East Fork—bear hunts—volcanic peaks and white summits—the huge gulf of the Grand Canyon, Warm Spring Creek below, Washburn Hot Springs, Canyon-Tower Road, Dragon's Mouth Spring, Mud Geyser, Yellowstone Lake—swampy regions flooded, myriads of water fowl.

Sand colors: Obsidian and minute crystals known as 'California Diamonds'—Bluestone Springs, Rainbow, Emerald and Green Pools, Castle Geyser, Giant Geyser, Grotto Geyser, Fan Geyser, fireworks and a gigantic fountain over 500 feet high—Madison Junction, camp sites and camp fires—en route to Virginia City, Come! Rush! Hurry!

Horse thieves, lawless men, drifters and gunslingers, ranch houses, saloons and people reading the *Western Monthly, the Overland Monthly, The Ladies' Home Journal, the Police Gazette, the Helena Daily Herald.*

Trout fishing with grasshopper bait—Pocketknife surgery for the men—warm climate, frequent rains—Fern, thimble berries, lodgepole pines, Engelmann's spruce, douglas fir, limber pines, subalpine, whitebark pine, Rocky Mountain juniper, cottonwoods, wild flowers, yellow woka blossoms, geraniums, lupines, phacelia, sunflowers, balsamroot, fringed gentian, cinquefoil.

West Thumb Geyser Basin, snowy water, bright pink mud—colors varying from pure white to dark yellow—everywhere deposits of red green yellow and black—purple waters. Blues and golds carried away by the wind, a drop of fire in the silence, petrified souls, silent prayers—forest fires—Geyser Black Sand Basin, Sunset Lake, Firehole River, A TRIP TO YELLOWSTONE NATIONAL PARK, poetry in topaz-colored mists—fur traders, lawmakers, surveyors, settlers and townsmen.

Ears of Indian corn groaning under the snow plows—minarets of emeralds and flowers—the American colors murmur to the stars.

Humor and courage dress history and its rumors, the rest simmers
in the libraries and the archives of Death TV—neon bubbles jostle
the film flowing as unchanging as a river rushing into the hallways
of the eye—micro-organisms exploding in the mirrors of the skull.

Memory crushes the garbage of time that piles up in stroboscopic
swirls, time's electric organ deforests empty heads and color-sounds
spell out: Boulder River, the Stillwater and Buffalo Jump, the sun
drops nearer the horizon and sets in the mirror of silence.

Rosebud Creek, Wagon Creek in Yankee Jim Canyon.

"During the night a cold blast blew up the valley and a sleet storm
came on after dark", you can still read on the yellowed paper:
"Washburn had the viewpoint of a surveyor", "The whereabouts
of Washburn's diary is unknown", "An interesting question is why
Walter de Lacy did not join the Washburn party", "Washburn
stood guard. Quite cold...Crow (Indians) near"—Herd of two
thousand elk lying in the snow, a bull moose stampedes the stock
—large flocks of pelican, mules and horses.

The Silent Language of the Plains—Custer's last message in a
moonless sky—after having killed him I buried the body of my
enemy in the sand, fire smoldered under the snow and his ashes
rose like cloud-snakes towards the Kingdom of the Dead.

Colorless timeless smoke—Barbershop Quartets—A Sioux vision:
"Go to the mountaintop and cry for a vision"; Nez Percé song:
"Mad Coyote madly sings, then the West wind roars"—Grand Tet-
on Country, Mad River Canyon—black ousel (water canary), my-
riads of birds, residents and seasonal migrants.

Bison, elk, muledeer, moose, bighorn, antelope, black bear and
grizzlies, coyotes, wolves, cougars, white-tailed deer, wolverines,
mink, badgers, weasels, martens, beaver, otters, skunks and mar-
mots—wild flowers growing like stars in the snow—the Tetons
on a moonlit night—Keenan City, Caribou Mining District, Fort
Hall, Falls Creek, Eagle Rock Bridge.

Bucks teeth are reflected in the eyes of the men responsible for

so many deaths—broken weapons, honey, gall, absent roses—our
God has doomed the dead frozen worlds where shoulderless men
multiply—wild flowers prove to us that the Universe isn't empty.

Yonder forest gay and smiling again wears its native hue; and the
meadows look beguiling tinged with lovely violets blue—day is
breaking, embers dance in the chimney, the wind grabs a dream-
less sleep, everything is perfect, bird language wrings screams, jade
and turquoise are born again in a feast of flames: COME! RUSH!
HURRY! DON'T WAIT FOR ANYTHING!

NOTE: *Quotes from:* 'BATTLE DRUMS AND GEYSERS' *by Orrin H. &
Lorraine Bonney, published by* The Swallow Press Inc. Chicago. Sage
Books. *'The Life and Journals of Lt. Gustavus Cheney Doane, Soldier and
Explorer of the Yellowstone and Snake River Regions'.* (Washburn's notes,
3000 words published by *The Helena Daily Herald*).

Weather: Frigid

*There was nothing routine about the
weather report issued last week by Vi-
king Meteorologist Seymour Hess. It was
the first ever from the planet Mars:*

"Light winds at 15 m.p.h., shifting
as any sensible wind is supposed to do.
Temperatures Tuesday ranging from a
low of −122° F. to an early afternoon
high of −22° F. and pressure of 7.70 mil-
libars." There was no precipitation re-
port: it has not rained on Mars for eons.

FADED HEARTS SHADOW-SINGERS & B SERIES

1

The shadow stirs the blue
of every sea.

2

Silences tied to mirages.
Poisoned rivers
are lost in the polychrome
mist——throng syllables
crushed, lynched key-images,
murdered children——a puff
of pure gold dissolved on the pavement.

3

Last dance——the wind
rises on the ancient ruins
of Silver City——the wind
devours the sky, fire runs
on the earth, it's raining
in the echo-chamber,
it's raining on the city.

4

A flexible sound
bursting from a silent
nightmare—a white twisted
fairy comes out of the water——
a vague image on the baggage
wagon, broken figures wander
in the halls of the airport.

5

Faded hearts, shadow-singers
& B series, a tornado of light
animates silver fingers
buried in the quagmire

of minced meat. Aluminum wires
linked to human targets
to eyes-under glass. Tonight
the voices of the wind track
moths in the fields
decayed by sobs.

NOTES

Soundlessly, wordlessly in eye-cages. On the instrument panel
the reflections of the sky and the headlights have taken refuge
within the pages of an old Bible Mary gave me——and sea foam on
Time's chopping-block——bees, in the moonlight, devour cancelled
stamps pinned onto the clouds.

The wind carries to us the smell of a wood fire and the barking of
a dog——soundlessly, wordlessly I open fire——several blasts ring
out, their eyes pop out and their monochrome sexes tremble in
the dust——their ripped stomachs puke liquids and victuals and
chipped scented memory-rings.

It's raining. Night is near. Seagulls fly over windswept cliffs——
the golden broom sets the horizon on fire——below, the river swol-
len by the rains smothers the sounds of the city.

Yesterday a pale sun lit up the somber valley, the rain blurred the
hills, people hurried along in the damp streets, haunted by the
dense fog and dead souls.

Friday/Saturday
while night
carved the shadow-sounds

PEBBLES IN THE SKY

1

Scattered screams,
masters of silence.
Debris-realities,
archipelagoes of pride
flaming in the warm
night—souvenirs
of Africa (edible)
(long after)—
life is nothing
but a dream, the Autumn mist
protects phantoms.

2

Oceans of wrinkles,
Electric Zodiac,
'Apache Juke', Dawn
the only conceivable
logic.

3

Almond-sounds breaking
faces of hate.

4

Hurricanes of screams
& laughter, terror
on North Main St.
Above the fields
of flowers mad
shadows wink
at moonbeams.

5

Veins spatter themselves
with spittle, hate impaled

on TV antennae
in Echo Park. Frost
collapses. Precipices
of TV flashes.

6

Scalpel-words
& French values
still play
on the fog-chessboard.

7

Here time
doesn't exist anymore.
Horizon-tatters
in the waves—
dream-tides
equinox-rapes.

8

Blood has shuffled
the cards, smoke-
ladders, spray,
fruity petals swallowed
by howling metal.

Wednesday/Friday
While a calm fire
tears this sequence apart

BONE-FREEZING BLUEPRINT

tickertape from Journals and short stories written at random

La vérité c'est pas mangeable
        —Louis-Ferdinand Céline

Just like this—but. . .
as 'Shoot-'em-up Mike' O'Malley says:
"It was the facts that formed my opinion,
Sir, nothing else but the *facts!*"

When I make a mistake it's a whopper!
        —Colonel Washburn pissing in the Pee Dee River

New voices are always found busy in strange places.
        —Chas Plymell

—it's too human, it's not
    human
It's treetops, whatever they think,
It's me, whatever I think,
It's the wind talking.
        —Allen Ginsberg

IT'S STILL THE SAME OLD STORY
A FIGHT FOR LOVE AND GLORY.

*

Indeed the facts remain, and these things are done. . .Blast-and-
Radiation, oh Lord! We're to be reduced to words. . .Of the
good old days nothing is left, everything is the color of mourn-
ing. . .great black birds wheel around the gallows. . .men with
their heads covered with red hoods swing in space—screams
tear thru the paleness of the dawn—a dazed populace is sub-
jected to infernal criminal machinations. . .children pass without
dreaming. . .blood flows in streets taken over by terrorists. . .sad
songs, pop*con,* a killer-vaudeville show—mauve flashes sear the
sky, faceless cameras film the quick and the dead.

*

The twins of space pose in their shiny suits. Our civilization is
dying inside a star—enemy agents seize your bodies minds and
souls—neon groans in the empty streets.

  People should be aware of their limitations, *that's* what liber-
ty is all about.

  A howl as a sign of farewell.

*

Echoes in the fog. . .poisoned echoes that haunt those who
were once repulsed by violence. . .VIOLENCE IS THE KEY—a
deathlike silence will spread over the Planet made alike from one
end to the other by little green men and red bureaucrats—the
sound of insects, hordes of cannibals, the great Organs of the
Gulag, the Peking Opera, the Bamboula, the Hitlerite Woodstock,
the Coming of the Ape. . .and the muffled murmurs of a totali-
tarian universe and concentration camps will replace the sounds
of life.

*

Riots still go on as planned.

  Chico Diaz screws in the bare bulb hanging from the ceiling
. . .dazed junkies puke blood in front of Bill Latimer's drug-
store. . .colored lights shine in every window, lightning flashes in

the low heavy sky. . .It's Christmas, merry Xmas!—a cold east
wind sweeps over vacant lots—ancient dreams in the headlights. . .
the city looks like a purple orange and ultraviolet brazier. . .red and
white lights dance up and down the highways. . .sexual impulses in
the cold damp air.

*

Electric news flickers on every screen—the North wind sweeps
the empty streets—ancient dreams take shape in the smoke.
    The streets shudder and take on color. Punks and hoodlums
come out of the overpopulated suburbs spreading terror and
shouting in the nigger streets.

*

Sodomy-suicide. Slow masturbations. Sickies and pervos kill
again and again—the mindless rabble comes out of the sewers of
hell and the time-tunnel—the XXIst century, the Twilight
World. . .fires in the distance. . .black disemboweled carcasses,
bleached skeletons crawling with flies and giant ants. . .magnes-
ium smoke in the sky.
    1999, Hamburger Hill. . .a merciless cold hate. . .a voice off
stage: "Long ago there was singing on the plantations"—cold
hate you can only see in a desperate and empty sky—excrement
evicted from the Archives of Death make the Simians squeal with
pleasure and come like rats in the sweet smelling blood shed in
the blue of the sky, coloring the raw light. . .colored images are
buried under the ruins. . .a merciless cold hate spread out in infinity.

*

NIETZCHE IS DEAD—signed: *God.*

*

The incurable procrastination of words weighs more and more
heavily on our destiny.

*

DON'T LOOK BACK! We've crossed every landscape, flown over
wide open spaces and speed has disfigured us, and we are fascin-
ated by prophecies and fantasies, subjugated by the Big Con, ob-

sessed by legends, we're daydreaming between heaven and earth, high and hypnotized by the Video Police and the Space Soap Opera. We were there at the end of the world, at the end of night, in the heart of the electrified slaughter. . .we wanted everything, here, fast now. . .we were wrong, we were betrayed, indeed the facts remain and these things are done—Shiva over-*macho*ing by Captain America has grown fat and shows his broken arm to everyone, Kali Yug's green and red eyes shine in the dark, Krishna has shed his skin with his dunce cap on, he's on Welfare, an anonymous groupie like the good doctor Turn-On—Lotus *vinaigrette'* sprays ammonia on the dance floor at the 'Thinking Hole', and a rain-fingered SOS blinks in the silver light of the blue and orange Galaxy.

*

Silent colors and famine pits.
  Day-Glo spectors and demons, shitfaced morons, silent films, sexes unfolded in Winchester recoils, and the Bodhisattwa dies on the butcher's block.

*

We came in from the cold, visible and invisible, light and carefree, free. We came in from the cold. We were elsewhere. We were from nowhere and everywhere like our ancestors, travelers, navigators, trappers, explorers, woodsmen, hunters, preachers, lawmen, outlaws, colonizers and settlers. We came in from the cold BUT NOT FROM ANYPLACE.

*

Burned photos. . .awful sounds in the metallic dawn. . .time-bites visible on a faded photo of James Dean. . .and Bix's silhouette behind the flames.

*

The Time-Guide climbs into a flying saucer in a shower of pink sparks and shards—dusty images in the eyes of a hanged man—Flashback: Earl closes his eyes, makes his vein swell and presses on the eyedropper. . .the fix dilutes the unclean foam where his gaze stagnates. . .he sighs, holds back a smile and lights a cigarette. . .the

dropper stares at him from the night-table, full of hate and death
...the message is clear——Orion Dream Stuff, quick-silver holes on
the black velvet of the sky——unmoveable, the oceans shake their
foam-sheets.

*

Flashback: ALL SNUFF-UNITS & THE ARYAN BROTHER
HOOD NETWORK ARE READY FOR THE CLASH/ALL SNUFF-
UNITS WILL DESTROY DEEP COVER AGENTS/THIS IS FOR
ALL TIME REAL...END OF MESSAGE——freckles, blond and
red hair on the vermillion sand at Anderson Creek——blood-stained
banners, musical comedy.

*

All Snuff-Units back from Death...Death on all fronts...
    Blasts from automatic weapons, explosions, fires, atrocities, po-
groms——chopper patrols in the wild light of an August sky——ci-
cadas and crickets sing, train whistles in the distance, squeaky
rock 'n' roll, faraway suicides...colored death and time-bites in
the empty streets.

*

James Dean is alive and well and working in a Branch of Barclay's
Bank in Swampshit City.

*

Flashback: I see Frisco in filigree...1963...Phil Whalen, placid
with a mischievous silent smile in front of a glass of wine...Snyder
with the weatherbeaten face busy with his incredible motorcycle
...McClure nervous and elegant forever combing his hair, a Bio-
Classic stroking September blackberries. . .A juiced up Lew Welch
gesticulating and joking. . .I see them all again in the moving fron-
tiers of lines, forever aggressed by the daily grind and politics——
Poets have no power, I say, Jimmy Fish-Tail then says I am a
Fascist, well, uh, so be it, but not a Fascist like the others——The
wind howls thru the screens of old photos and in the pages of old
anthologies——dangerous maniacs surround us and tempt us...What
to do? I've no idea, I only have personal reactions...I see Gins-
berg again at the Hot Dog Palace jacking off God's Eye and talking

to Mme Nhu; and Ferlinghetti looking over his unionized Beatniks'
pay checks (a free thought, pal, after all and thank God art is bus-
iness, big business). . .Duncan with his great black cape gliding sil-
ently on the sidewalk. . .Kaufman and McClaine slobbering in the
neon lights of Broadway in front of the Jazz Workshop. . .Janine
and Huncke scoring, and all the others happy or sad, carefree or
desperate, one and all forgotten today, erased sick dead and/or re-
habilitated, even more desperate because neither life nor the world
have changed—electrified flesh in the inevitable exploding plastic
of New York, spark-cradles, colorful dreams longer than the night
—evil flowers, tortured bodies, deranged minds, annihilated geni-
uses and sages trampling the guts of nothingness.

*

PEOPLE AND PLACES—Sinbad, Charlie Chan, Modesty Blaise,
Rip Kirby, Flash Gordon, Dick Tracy, El Floppo, Hawkman, The
Camel, Wonder Woman, Supermonkey, Society John, Superdog,
The Green Lantern, Jimmy the Fink, Perfume Jack, Clifton de
Berry, Rose Nebraska, Panama Joe, Arizona Clark, Lola Pozo,
Diarrhea Montez, Spiderman, Cohen-Cohen & Cohen Inc., Johnny
Pissoff, the Trashman, Suzy Creamcheese, Randy Redneck, the
Masked Cucumber, the Venusian Banana, Stinking Cloud, Crazy
Jap, Howling Metal & Old Lace, Charlotte the Red, the Mad Anti-
Semite, the Recycled Wog, Zorba the Shmuck, Chopstick Charlie,
Jose Bravo, Shit-on-a-Stick the one-legged nigger, Papa Nosedrop,
Johnny Guitar, the Musical Sleeping-Bag, the Catatonic Hippie,
Moe Bercovici, Dr. Mind-Fucker and the Cosmic Whore. . .the In-
terplanetary Police went thru the demoniac screen and crashed in-
to a grey wall. . .electronic stoolies hidden on the corner of Caro-
lina and Elm Streets. . .From NATO with love. . .Johnny Handsome
and Jimmy Smart are still playing Black Jack. . .a Mandrake convul-
sion in the heart of this puzzle crushed under the wheels of the
Snow Subway. . .Juju, Chano Pozo, Johnny Cool, Tom & Ray,
Machinegun Kelly, Jimmy Fish-Tail, Scruffy-Ass Nigger, Jim Mc-
Bain, Himmler, Amanda, Jefferson, the 'Cold Summer of 1816',
Greenwood, Silver City, the Space Civic Center, the Sperm Hotel,
Butcherknife Bill, Alesbury Road, Honolulu, Neuva Chicago, Misty
Sink, Anderson Creek, Isaac Stern, Colonel Ryan, Sgt. O'Malley,
Ed the Coffin, Pollux, Mrs. O'Connell, Mrs. Himes, Fat Jack Mc-
Nabb, Mitchell, Mr. Bradford, Jackson-Walk-Too-Fast, Rusty Jack,

The Finger-Eaters and the Red Dykes, Honey Boy Bongo, Mrs.
O'Brien, Judge Parker, Judge Slim Butter from Dodge City, 23rd
Street, Lenox Avenue, Taylor Street, the Highway Patrol, the
SWAT, the President, Paco from Pig Alley, Billy, Charlie the Gook,
Dirty Face Charlie, Joe Verminex, Papi Tomato, 'Chez Luigi', The
Sandy Toes Motel, the Swim 'n' Swing Motel, the 'Wives & Whores',
the 'Guys & Dolls', Missouri Dale, Sally Harmony, Sheriff 'Punk'
Jones, Disneyland, Mme Kitty, Sam Spade, Johnny Dollar, Deadly
Mother Duncan, the Great Western Hotel, William Buckley, Jr.
and John Wayne, Death Row Jeff, the Snuff Units, the Video Pol-
ice, the Time Guides, the Dream Police, UFO Watergate, Colonel
Washburn, Old Mint Street, Jeff Kissass Morton, Black Maria, Miles
End Road, Bill Latimer, Gun Hill, Pee Dee River, Hamburger Hill,
Firehole River, Neurotic Beach, Johnny Hale, Oak Street, Molly O'
Dwyer, Gene O'Neil, Sam Whiteson, Old Angel Midnight, Death
Badge Jay, Jessica, Mad Mary Maddox, Stephanie, Flash Tattoo,
Jenkins, Doc Holiday, T-Bone Charlie, Uncle Tacos, Harry Lon-
baugh, Nick Silverhead, Kitty Teagarden, the Pizza Squad, Mama
Sutra and Pretty Boy Floyd, John Dillinger, Dr. Feelgood, Mr. Fix-
it, Mr. Motto, Soddy Slim Moddy, Blue Pete Keeler, Ben Pigass
Thompson, Dracula, Billy Wickup, Golda Schwartzenberg, Chero-
kee Bill, Sam Crosby, Moe Goldberg, Maple Street, Mantra Chickie,
the Video Rangers, Yellow Hair Morgan, Rainbow Hill Expressway,
Juan Rodriguez, Ursula, the Church of Satan, Dan Pepper, the Vid-
eotheque of the Universe, The Bionic Chicken, the FBI, Willy and
Joe, the Simians, Avenida Solitario, the Rainbow Studio, Zipper
Puke, Bodega Bay, Big Sur, Julius Hoffman, Karen K., Primrose
Hill, the Great Galactic Ghoul, the Chasm Gang, the Sexual Prole-
tariat, Snag Pie Town, Dan Pepper, Line Camp David, Clovis,
Prairie Town, Sol Danda, Zim and Groonsberg, O'Brien, Ben Gay,
Sister Vaseline, the Kosher Cowboy, Bud Barrow, the Oriental Baz-
aar, the Pope, the Survival Room, Trask Cable, Father O'Neil, the
Greenspan Bros, the Land of the Dead, Cong Foey, Ida, Division
West, the Wet Dream Showboat, Gasoline Alley, Deer Lodge Val-
ley, the 'Moth & Flame', Jack & Sutter, the Buena Vista, the NET-
WORK, the KKK, the CIA, the Aryan Brotherhood, the Red Cross,
the USMC, California Street, Patchwork Boulevard, Ike, the Red
Alert, Da Nang, Cam Ranh Bay, Saigon, Mr. Moreno, the Syndicate,
Mr. O'Hara, Grand Central, the Pentagon, the *Nigger Review*, Lady
Pamela, the Vice Squad, Liberty Lane, Carter Brown, Eddie, Tom,

Larry and Lou. Mrs. Morton, Chickie Fly Tox, Mr. Earp, Chad and
Chuck, Bella Kuntz, Wavy Gravy, W.O.G. Files, Ronald Craddock,
Interpol, Chester Grey, Fagola Street, the KGB, Mario the Guinea,
the Beebee Club, Limpy Scholtz, the DA, David Blum, Murder Inc.,
Stan Levy, the Kike Ko-op, Last Chance Charlie, Hooker Row, Dr.
Szabo, Dr. Ratman, Cerise Darling, Fort Knox, the Sperm Bank,
the Swift Kick Operation Mind Fuck Inc., the Oriental Warfare Private
Corporation, the Chemical and Biological Snuff Units, the Institute
of Paranormal Births, the Emergency Operation Center, Captain
James Brooks, Mad Dog County, Nigger Ben Hill, Smackass Pass,
the Ginger Connection, Teresa Broom, Billy Yank, Jay West, Mud
River, West Thumb Bridge, Carroll Road, Duff Cooper, David St.
John, High Chaparral, the Blowtorch Castration Squad, Benny
Davis, la Belle Eugène, Angela Curler, Dave Jocko, the Texas Ace,
the 'Barrio', Niggertown, John McCabe, the *rue Sans Joie,* the
NASA, the *rue des Longs Couteaux,* Technopolis, Assfuck City,
Chico Diaz, Julius Nathan, Tijuana, L.A., Frisco, Market Street,
Maricones Plaza, the Royal Armpit Hotel, the DEA, the UN, Dr.
Snow, Lord Selwood, Brian and Stew, TPF Decoy Squad, Clancy
Morgan, Liam Blackwater, Juana Gomez, the 'We Belonged West',
Will Jenkins, Arrowhead Street, Christopher Street, Mariposa
Street, Magical Street, the Cliff House Hotel, the Seaside Hotel,
Molly Gaines, the Pink Mermaid, the Pink Window, Winterbottom
Road, Eva Moore, Stringybark Street, Main Street, Jim Diamond,
Harry Buster and Al Watkins, Jesus Chavez the Spider, High Street,
Troy Kulak, Felipe Cantina, Mr. Big, Pepe Amadeo, Rattlesnake
Bill, Mr. McClure, Bernie Blum IV, Lucy Mirror, Sgt Fury, the
Dixie Flutes, the Feds, the Zionist Asshole, Lord Jim, the Palestin-
ian Insect, the Malaria Merchant, River Street Fish Market, the
Piss Factory, Pepe the Moko, Colonel Haigh, the Blue Planet Note-
books, Pacific Grove, Red Wing River, the Rubber Lips Marchin'
Band, the Death Squad, Meat Package Inc., Death Row Paradise,
Dr. Goebbels, Manson & Family, the Gulag, Mrs. Sundance and
the Juicy Fruit Kid, the Blue Kid, Mad Sister Louise, the Nuns of
Manza, the Villains of Space, etc. . .indeed the facts remain *and
these things are done*—

*

I was strolling on the boardwalk photographing dead and living
writers.

That day I noticed that it was the end of mankind, that moral
decay was attacking everything.

Tuberculous sperm shining in the Spring sunlight. The down
and out wander in a blurred world.

Remote sounds die in cafeterias.

Bright spots and Father Brown are stoned by youths armed
with broken bottles.

Mr. Has-Been cultivates lovely roses in his garden on Long Island,
'Perry Como' roses.

The fragrant twilights of quiet days in New England and Florida
so close to the stars.

The quiet days, parks, garden parties, strolls in the forest along
the banks of the river, hunting and fishing far away from the toxic
images and stenches of the rabble.

People understand with horror that there is nothing to be done.
The silence is shattered by blood curdling voices.

Songs gallop in the heads of little people. I fall asleep at the
wheel of the Buick. I dream. A football match—I drift thru the
moon—the hideous scars have gone—I inhale the aroma of the
roses.

*

A shot, a blinding flash and a strong ghetto-odor flies from hand to
hand. Damp flakes on the black and vermillion sands of Dare Devil
Creek.

Snow-covered bandstands.

Shots in a side street, blood spurting to the sky.

Torn velvet curtains. The smell of sweat, factories and excre-
ment. Laments and groans.

Nightmare images hang from the metal pylons. Images rush at
random in streets and alleyways. Remote colors expire in the
opaque clouds.

The evil film crashes against a child's laughing eyes.

Crumpled streets, numb figures vanish thru the looking-glass.

*

Red anemones are broken by laser beams.

Showers of archives in the back-world.

*

A coyote snarls at Dare Devil Creek on top of the hill. Thru a curtain of mist you feel the fire that precedes the sun rise.
     You hear the hoarse cries of the biological and nuclear family being annihilated by perverts.
     A negress runs away in the bilious light chased by lesbians armed with cleavers and electric saws.
     Dying images in the blurred moonlight.
     Fade-in chained to the fires of hell.

*

The neon sign flickers at 'Heartbreak Hotel'.

*

Cicadas and crickets sing in the blue electric night.
     The heavy foliage is caressed by the warm night air on Carolina Avenue.
     Sprawled in his rocking chair old Jefferson picks the strings of his guitar and his wife sings the Blues. . . 'Blues My Naughty Sweetie Gave To Me'.

*

The razor pukes furtive clinches.
     Death on all fronts. Dust-mosaics. Black snow falls on the faded mirror of time.
     Black Molly, the woman with the fog-eyes weeps as she stares at the star-spangled asphalt of sickness.

*

From every angle reality becomes more and more sordid. Neon, a prisoner of fog blinks over the movements of the crowd.

*

Crimes, rape, aggression, hold-ups, mob-fights, hi-jackings, murder by death——at high noon a man is stabbed in front of the Chinese laundry on 23rd Street——"Strange", murmurs Sgt. O'Malley a.k.a. 'Shoot-'em-up' Mike——*strange* indeed, you anticipate everything, put everything in order, you're sure of everything except what can happen to you, and things only *really* change when you risk your life *knowingly.*

*

Death Brown Horse floods the streets of NY. All you can hear are
the sirens of police cars and ambulances.
   That day I trembled in front of the fearsome muzzle of a .38
under a dizzy sky of stars and neon lights.
   It is cold. I shiver. Is it fear? Loneliness? Overwork? Dis-
gust? Despair? I dunno—life maybe, yes, I think just life itself.

*

Between life and death on the path of blood there is only room
for the living.

*

The moon is rising in the silvery mist.
Clouds scud along flush with the horizon.
   Night swallows the hills overlooking the city. The mist seems
to gasp in a neon-reddened mouth. *Our Lady of Sorrows.*

*

Debris of winter twilight around a hallucination-world, sweep life,
things and people away, to and fro. Debris of gallows and electric
chairs, polar crockery sits on the feline odor of night.
   DOA—Yes sir! Died in the line of duty—"Drop dead New
York!" screamed the headlines of the Daily News—July, 85°F,
100% humidity, a fiery furnace. A yellow haze asphyxiates Man-
hattan—wild iris sizzle in carbon dioxide claws. On 5th Avenue
white roses turn the colors of vitiated blood—soot is diluted on
faces by a fine drizzle as well as sweat and metallic dust. Potted
ferns turn brown as if mutilated by the pincers of frost, and yet
it is summer—Puerto Rican mucus drips over everything.

*

I feel like going to Florida for a rest or to New England—to see
the maples, oaks, elms, birches, horses, hills, country roads and
people, human beings.

*

Here murders à gogo—a car drives by all lights out, a packet of

dynamite tossed out of the window—a terrific explosion—
Machinegun Suzy vanishes screaming thru the quick silver screen,
silently the heavy magenta curtain at the 'Pink Cloud' was ripped.

*

Terrible noises in the heart of the anecdote.
　　Dramas erased by the last April snows.
　　A swell of sounds odors and stutterings—a few more words
about dead flesh—heavy sour smells in the Snow Subway—the
Dream-Police is watching and a flood of neon erases the whole
story.
　　Murderers have no age.

*

The history of mankind is a subtle moan—junkies fade in the
grey dawn and always tell the same story—there is nothing more
to say.

*

Night overflows from dawn to dusk.
　　Agony to breathe here says Chano Pozo, and the smell didn't
seem to bother anyone.

*

Rose Nebraska picked up the crumbs of an old western.

*

Arizona Clark dug his phosphorescent nails into 'Death Row' Jeff's
stringy flesh.
　　The film burns slowly.
　　Cities are cold and hungry.
　　Loud idiotic Rock 'n' Roll is broadcast in the loudspeakers of
Technopolis—sexy messages die late in the afternoon—In its es-
sential cruelty war is the same everywhere—more and more we
feel as if we're in danger.

*

Mosaic-Police—Brain-Dealers—moon debris beyond the call of

duty—Black Molly DOA—the polar horizon is dripping with
rain—Our Lady of Neon—mauve asphalt bitten by the Brain-Pol-
ice—everything's in order on 23rd Street, the Automatic Pilot
aims at Spanish Harlem's pale seams—Now I live in Pooh country
—that day I visited a Jewish hippie commune, mice and bugs
wore overalls—at high noon 'Shoot-'em-up' Mike strolled in the
debris of twilight—Death on all fronts—Silver City, a City of Il-
lusion, an earth-waring machine—snow blue with anger, reality
filled with sickness—an APB for another time—the odor of wild
beasts falls on the city—the debris of a life in the sky—sobs
smothered in time's dazed mouth—SOS, Station Caroline's faded
mirror doesn't answer anymore, death pierces space—nights are
swept by ice-laden winds—Murder by death—winter fogs creak
in the magenta reflections of sick images—fearsome noises in the
April snow—the Dream Police traffics in flesh—Rose Nebraska
and Missouri Dale follow Time-Guides in the Jewish columns of
the 'Daily News', dream after dream in the claws of the sun Mrs.
O'Connell's white roses fade—an ink-trip on the quick silver
screen.

*

Anecdotes are torn up in silence and floods of neon erase daily
tragedies—a world in pieces dissolves slowly—sexy messages are
trampled in the washrooms frequented by faggots and smut ped-
dlers hidden behind Emerald City's propaganda screen—old
photos spell out the word 'C-r-u-e-l-t-y'—human beings and mad
Simians haunt the halls of the Snow Subway and junkies and per-
vos fade in the ethereal blue of space—a star spangled rainbow of
tragedy—assassins cough—echoes of live flesh howl on the razor's
edge.

*

Time-Guides chased by the Villains of Space fade into a jungle of
old photos.

*

The first glimmers of dawn race down hills and canyons and the
wild icy wind sweeps the top of the hill and whistles in the branch-
es of the old gnarled oak trees, and Judge Parker's stomach surges.

The prisoners' lower lips tremble, they look fearfully around.

Billy W... shits in his pants, tears of rage and impotence spurt from his eyes.

The sheriff's deputies advance with coiled ropes that they throw over the highest branches. They curl gracefully around the frost-covered black wood. They make five nooses and tighten each knot with precise gestures.

In the distance the church bell rings.

The condemned men raise their eyes. The crowd breathes hard. Frozen, Shivering. Silent.

The wind howls.

The five men realize there is no hope, and that it isn't the first time hoodlums are hanged in Misty Sink.

*

The men's necks crack in unison when the pickup truck drives off. Their legs dangle in space, quivering hunting for support—Blue Pete Keeler struggles for a long time then suddenly he relaxes.

The crowd sighs. Then there is a long silence on top of Gun Hill, and for an instant the wind dies down.

The five bodies swing to and fro like huge pendulums.

Judge Parker stares up at the great branches. The sheriff studies the hanged men.

The spectators leave in small groups, talking about their affairs, avoiding the subject of the execution.

*

The wind blows more violently. Snow flakes swirl around. It is daylight now. You can see the black waters of Red Wing River in the distance.

*

A panic-wind whistles in Happy Valley. The thick snow squeaks under our boots. We would atone for our sins in blood. God had forsaken us.

*

Things unfold beginning with a shock but without this initial shock nothing would count. Body-images steal away. The wind raises old papers. A tragic light spreads over the world. Where is night made? God falls back flickering in a fog of blood.

*

Castrated the West groans under the light's skin. More and more the past plays an important role in fiction.

*

We visited a hippie commune. Nauseating. Barely mature junkies are on the nod sitting in their own excrement. Young girls are shooting up in their wombs. *One easy way to the grave, mister.*

*

The human thing is war.

*

A deliberate action conceived by intelligent beings. Violence is the key—sexual guerrilla warfare in the streets of the world.

*

As eternity is a long weekend and the past a foreign land, when I get back to earth centuries will have rolled by.

*

Old punks die hard. This line is the story of that death.

*

Dingbat nig nogs jack off in the orange neon light, laser-cameras rip up the ocean-planet.
    The ashes of this old Western are scattered by electronic fairies.

*

We're still in time. We're not in space.

*

Ladies and gentlemen the party's over. Pale silhouettes stagger in

the fog. Kiss your asses goodbye, shitheads! It was yesterday.
Shots in Old Mint Street. Dark Tides and Silent Speakers. Killing
at Gun Hill Railroad Station. A muffled rumbling rises near the
Charles Manson International Airport. The past is a foreign land.
The Shiran-Shiran Stadium is gone.

I was with the President on the terrace. We were drinking rum
'n' coke. We smoked in silence.

A shooting star streaked across the sky.

The smell of gunpowder and blood. Inert bodies on the floor
strewn with spent cartridges. Then silence. Washburn smiles as he
puts his winchester back on the rack.

*

The President's dick dropped off that's all.

*

Splintered blinds and shutters banged in the wind.

Thank God we had remained men.

Men were about to die. Flesh-petals swirl in the sky mixing
with the snow flakes Helicopters take off in the cold, sparkling
in the pale winter sunlight.

*

The First Lady kneels in the vomit and prays.

*

Horrible images pushed on by the great voices of the past.

A throng eagerly awaits blood and image-bodies.

The Time-Guides run into the exigencies of daily life: to shit,
piss, fuck, drink, eat, die. The sick flesh of contaminated surviv-
ors rots in the pink radioactive foam.

*

A unit of Marines in Old Mint Street pushed back hypnotized hys-
terical natives.

Moe Goldberg is lynched in front of his own pawnshop.

*

Metallic phantoms wander in the mist and dislocated bodies hang from the highest branches, old papers and dust are reflected in our pale eyes.

*

Missouri Dale, cold and stiff is laid out in the middle of the room with her skirt raised above her knees, her face all blue.

*

The wind is wilder and wilder raising cellophane wrappings, old newspapers and steel dust.
   Bunker Hill and Pee Dee River have fallen into the hands of the rebels.

*

Brilliant painful things pass to and fro in front of 'Death Badge' Jay's eyes.

*

The survivors devour each other, eat grass, fight over daffodil and hyacinth bulbs. Others copulate like animals at the edge of the pool which is overflowing with urine and excrement.

*

Females devour male sexes. Plastic dongs were grafted on some of them. Death bugged out of their eyes. Behind the blurred horizon the biological family was dying. Nothing held mankind to life.

*

The shadows were lengthening. The sky was turning pale.

*

The melting snow looked like a necklace of tears. Raw lights danced on the horizon.

*

Taking a photo just when the ropes stiffened. A sinister cracking.
The condemned man let out a terrible cry. His neck was distended,
ligaments, veins and flesh burst apart. A huge purple tongue dan-
gled out of his mouth. Polaroid cameras flashed.

*

The 'Green Eyes Machine' faced civilized fears.
    Buzzards wheeled around in the sky.

*

When it's a question of space you must change your way of think-
ing, is what the President kept saying.

*

Something exploded in the President's brain.
    Words fell endlessly. The film unwound, the tapes were burn-
ing.

*

God! We're going to live thru it.
    Two hours went by.

Deep End
Razor Burn Station
Over Silver City

$3.50

Cherry Valley Editions
Box 303
Cherry Valley,
NY 13320